I Love to Dance

I Love to Dance

to

Dance

a true story about Tony Jones

by Gerry Zeck

Carolrhoda Books, Inc. • Minneapolis

Many people have helped me with this book. Most of my appreciation goes to my friend Anthony Thomas (Tony) Jones, whose active life was the inspiration for *I Love to Dance*! May you dance forever, Tony. Thanks also to Bill and Ginny Jones. I am grateful to the School of the Minnesota Dance Theater and to Becky Stanchfield, Marcia Chapman, and Loyce Houlton. Additional help came from Sylvia Bolton and Mark Lynch of the Children's Theater Company. The Lakeshore Players were wonderful. Thanks to Bobby Crabb for opening his class. Frank Bourman offered valuable criticism on the first draft of the book. Thanks to Kathie Goodale for permission to use photographs (pages 8-9 and 62) from *Pas de Trois*. And a final thanks to Susan Pearson, my editor, for her faith and her patience.

Manufactured in the United States of America

Designed by Gale Houdek

LIBRARY OF CONGRESS CATALOGING IN PUBLICATION DATA

Zeck, Gerry.
   I love to dance!

   Summary: Ten-year-old Tony Jones describes
his dance classes, the performances he's been
in, and his ambitions for the future.
Illustrated with black-and-white photos.
   1. Jones, Anthony Thomas—Juvenile
literature. 2. Dancers—United States—
Biography—Juvenile literature. [1. Dancers]
I. Title.
GV1785.J54Z4   793.3'2'0924 [B] [92]   82-4232
ISBN 0-87614-198-X   AACR2

1 2 3 4 5 6 7 8 9 10 87 86 85 84 83 82

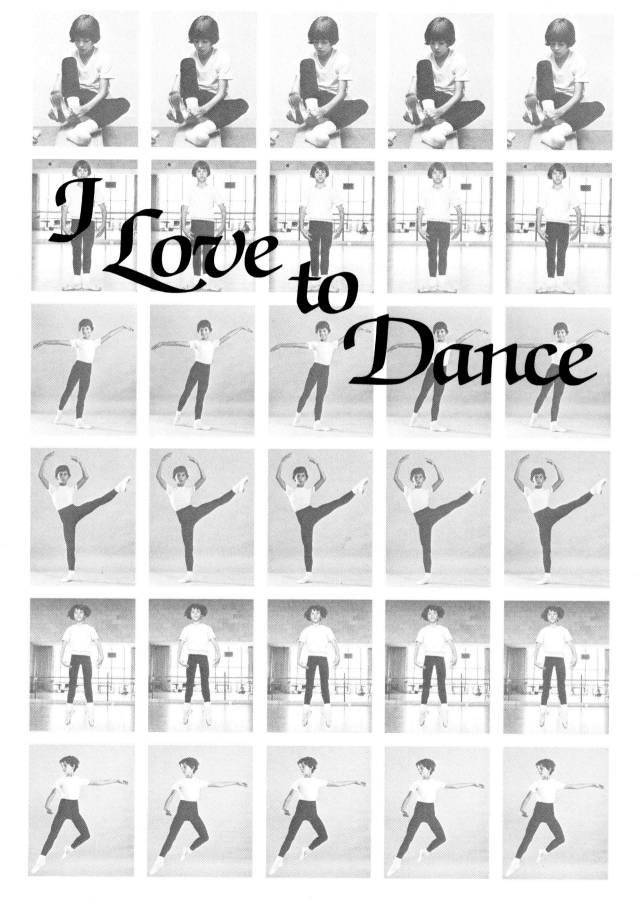

I Love to Dance

For Adrian

I love to dance more than anything else.

I'm Tony Jones. I'm ten years old and I study dance at the School of the Minnesota Dance Theater in Minneapolis. When I grow up, I want to be a dancer with the American Ballet Theater in New York City.

When I was eight years old, I was in a play called *The Music Man*. Becky Stanchfield was the choreographer for the play. She teaches dance at the School of the Minnesota Dance Theater. She asked me to take lessons at MDT, and so I did.

The School of the MDT has two divisions. The Preparatory Division is for beginning dancers. After you are nine years old, you can audition to join the Performing Arts Division. When you get into Performing Arts, you get to perform in *The Nutcracker* and in the annual Children's Dance Theater Workshop.

When I was nine, I auditioned to get into the Performing Arts Division. I auditioned every day for a week. Then I waited for my letter. Finally it arrived. I'd made it!

This year I'm taking two ballet classes and two contemporary dance classes every week. Right now I'm on my way to Becky's ballet class.

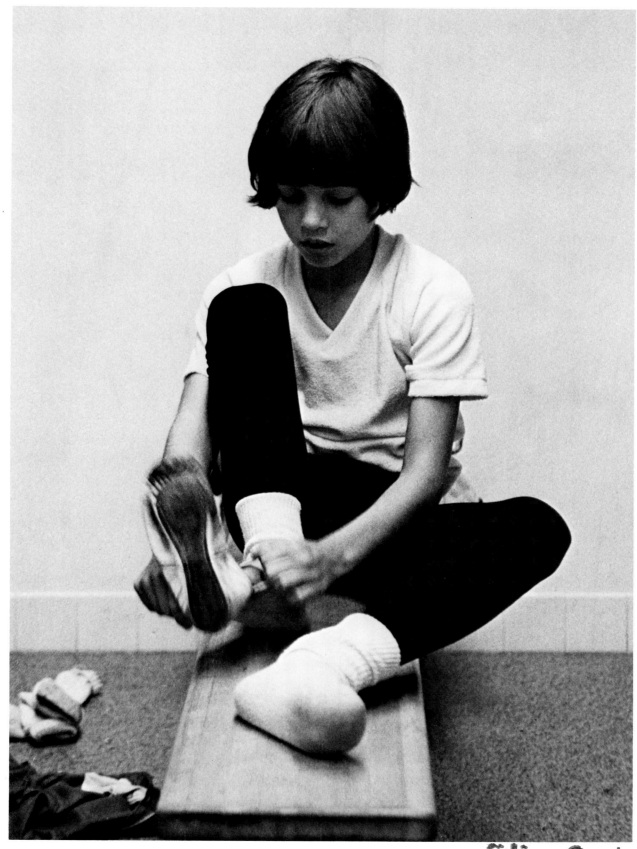

Becky starts each class with a special exercise. We
sit quietly on the floor. We forget about other things.
We think only of being here.

Slowly our muscles relax. Our breathing becomes easier. Finally we are ready to dance.

All ballet lessons start at the *barre* (bar). We hold the *barre* for support while we warm up our muscles.

Becky calls out the names of exercises in French, and we do them. Like all dancers, we practice the same movements again and again.

At the *barre* the inside leg is called the supporting leg. The outside leg is the working leg.

Ballet is a special form of dance that combines dance movements with music and theater. Most of the ballet steps we use in class were made up 200 to 300 years ago in France. Today we still use French words to describe the steps of ballet.

I must learn what perfect form looks and feels like.
My arms and my legs are like the branches and
roots of a tree. The trunk of my body must be
positioned just right so that my arms and legs will
be perfectly balanced. Perfect form is the goal of
all ballet dancers.

First Position

The first thing I learned in ballet class was how to stand like a dancer. A ballet dancer stands with knees and toes pointing out to the sides. Standing like this balances the trunk of the dancer's body.

Next I learned the five positions of ballet. These positions are very important. All ballet steps begin and end in one of these positions.

Second Position

Third position looks a lot like Fifth Position. It isn't used very much in ballet anymore.

Fourth Position

Fifth Position

Sometimes I feel something like a ball of energy
in the pit of my stomach. That warm ball is the
center of my body. When I exercise, I work to find
my center. It is my place of balance.

I must become flexible in all parts of my body and
mind. When I am older and my legs are very strong,
I will build the strength of my upper body. I will
lift weights until I am strong enough to lift ballerinas
into the air.

Some boys don't take dance lessons because so many girls dance. I am not so shy. When a few kids at school teased me about dancing, I didn't let it bother me. Dancing makes me feel good, and I want to be a dancer more than anything in the world.

After we have warmed up at the *barre*, we move
to the center of the dance floor. Here we do jumps
and turns and combinations of dance steps that need
a lot of space. Here is where the fun of dance really
begins.

A male dancer in a ballet company is called a *danseur* (dahn-SER). The *premier danseur* (PREHM-yay dahn-SER) is the leading, or principal, male dancer in the company. *Danseuse* (dahn-SOOZ) is French for female dancer. The principal female dancer in a ballet company is called either a *premiere danseuse* (PREHM-yair dahn-SOOZ) or, in Italian, a *prima* (PREE-muh) *ballerina*.

We line up in rows so that we can study our
movements in the mirror. By studying our reflections
we can begin to see how we might look to an audience.
The longer you dance, the more you are able to
notice in the mirror.

On Saturdays I take contemporary dance lessons
from Marcia Chapman. Contemporary dance is
different from ballet. For one thing, we don't wear
shoes during our lessons. For another, we don't
warm up at a *barre*. Instead we start with warm-ups
in the middle of the dance floor. We want to learn
to move our bodies from one position into another
with speed and balance.

Today we are practicing prancing like horses. Next week we will prance on stage in the school's annual dance performance.

At the end of the school year, each student receives
a letter from the teacher. When I got my letter
from Marcia, I opened it in a hurry. It made me
smile. It said that I had passed on to the next level
in the Performing Arts Division.

Everyone in Performing Arts gets to take the
Children's Dance Theater Workshop. The Workshop
was started by Loyce Houlton, the founder of MDT.
We are working on our annual dance performance
which is called, *Licorice and Giblets, or Once Upon
a Folktale, or Just a Crazy Moment*. Mrs. Houlton
guides each dancer as we create our own dances.
We attend cast meetings and dance rehearsals just
like a ballet company preparing for a big performance.

Loyce Houlton is a famous choreographer. Her dances have been performed on stages all around the world. She knows how to create stage magic.

Everyone in Mrs. Houlton's workshop wants to work some stage magic during the performance of *Licorice and Giblets*. We've been workshopping hard every Saturday and Sunday for the past two months, and performance time is almost here.

Mrs. Houlton says that one of the secrets of stage magic is hard work. She tells us that it's important to express ourselves in our dance. But, she says, we'll really begin to discover ourselves when we learn to dance with others, and that's another secret of stage magic.

One part of the performance that I am in is a "studio sketch" called *The Bremen Town Musicians*. It's based on a German folktale about four animals. I play the role of Chanticleer the Rooster. Amy is the donkey. Danielle plays Bruno, the old dog. And Lisa is Mistress Cat. We dance to the music of Johann Strauss.

It's exciting to dance for a big audience. We began practicing for these studio sketches in our classes at the beginning of the school year. Now each step we practiced time and time again in dance class becomes part of our performance. This is another secret of stage magic—practice.

After our performance, the school year at MDT is over, but I'm taking a summer ballet class at Children's Theater Company. My mom is driving in a car pool so I can get across town to take the lessons. My mother's name is Ginny Jones, and I

couldn't study dance without her. Mom is not only
my mother, she's my dance manager too. She backs
me up whenever I need help or encouragement. She
washes my dirty tights and helps me keep my
schedule straight.

Sylvia Bolton is the dance mistress at Children's
Theater Company and my teacher.

I took my very first dance lessons at Children's
Theater Company. That was about three years ago.
I was in a Children's Theater musical production of
The Legend of Sleepy Hollow. I played the role of
a schoolboy, and I was supposed to give the teacher

an apple. One time during a performance I dropped the apple into the orchestra pit. I almost cried.

At first I didn't like it at Children's Theater Company, but then I met Sylvia Bolton. She was also a dancer at MDT. And she was the best teacher I'd ever had. She showed me how much fun it is to dance.

Sylvia showed me ways to jump higher. She showed
me how to push off the floor with my whole foot.
I keep my heel on the floor and use my legs to
lift me off the ground.

The more I practice pushing off, the easier it
gets to jump. I love to jump and leap into the air.
Sometimes I just can't keep my feet on the ground.

When we work on jumps and turns, we start in the
far corner of the dance floor. When the music starts,
we dance in pairs toward the opposite corner. Once
everybody has crossed the floor, we return to the
corner we left. The diagonal path gives us a little

more dancing space, and dancing this way, we can see ourselves from both sides in the mirrors.

Some days I feel like I could stay in the air forever. That's when leaping is such great fun. That's when I'm feeling the happiest.

Sonja Kostich is my best friend. I call her Myrtle.
She calls me Turtle. We take dance lessons together
at Children's Theater, and our families even go on
summer vacations together. Whenever we talk to
each other, we talk about dance. Mikhail Baryshnikov
is my favorite dancer. Myrtle likes Yoko Ichino a lot.

I like to keep busy, even if I'm just waiting for something else to happen. So I often telephone Sonja to talk about dance or theater. Both of us like to act too. Acting and dancing are both performing arts, so the things we learn in one are always useful in the other.

I've always liked musicals, so I've always auditioned for roles in plays. It didn't bother me if I didn't get the part. I just had to try. When I was six years old, I auditioned for a play at the New Hope Community Theater. The play was *Oliver*, and I got in. I've acted in more shows since then, including *The Music Man*, *A Christmas Carol*, and *The Legend of Sleepy Hollow*.

Right now I'm waiting for Mark Lynch to drive me to Lakeshore Players, a community theater in White Bear Lake, Minnesota. Mark works for Children's Theater Company during the day, but he's the director of the Lakeshore Players' production of *The Fantasticks* at night. Tonight is the dress rehearsal.

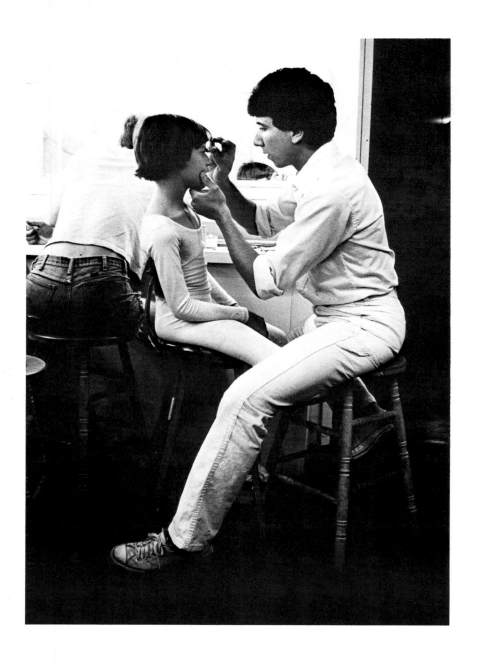

Mark applies my makeup for the dress rehearsal.
Makeup is an old tool of the actor. It's used to make
the features of the face more intense. On the stage
we use our voices, our bodies, and our faces to
deliver our lines, but sometimes our expressions
must be exaggerated because the audience is so
far away.

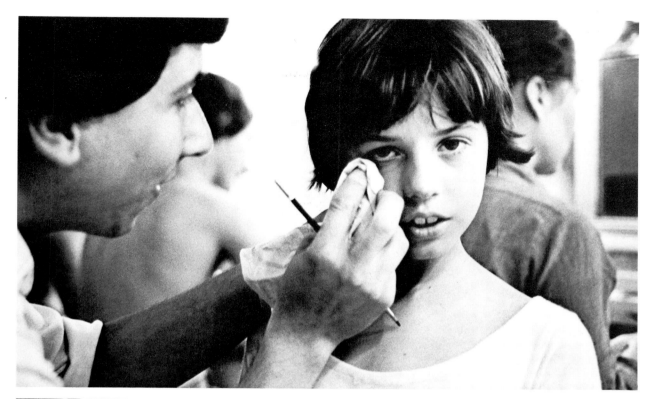

The Fantasticks is one of the most popular musicals of the American stage. It is a story about next-door neighbors. The fathers want their children to fall in love, so they build a wall between their houses and pretend to be enemies.

I play the role of The Mute. I don't have any lines to speak. Instead I am a mime. I open and close the two acts with a banner. Sometimes I become the wall between the neighbors. And I mime with a pinwheel when El Gallo and Luisa sing "Round and Round."

The Fantasticks has a lot of good music and a happy ending. We did nine performances of the play during July, and I had fun even though I was the only child actor in the cast.

Once in a while I take an adult ballet class at
Children's Theater Company. Dancing with adults
reminds me of my goal to become a dancer. It also
reminds me that I have a lot of hard work and
study ahead of me. For example, there are several
forms, or levels, of dance classes in the Performing
Arts Division at MDT. After I have completed
them all, there are a number of advanced programs
which lead to an apprenticeship with the Minnesota
Dance Theater.

Dancers love to dance. Even my teacher, Sylvia, continues to take dance lessons. In fact, the older and the stronger dancers get, the more they dance. By the time I'm fifteen years old, I'll be in two or three dance classes a day, seven days a week.

I'm just beginning to dance. That makes the future feel exciting. In the meantime, I have time for other things too.

THE WIZARD OF OZ

by L. Frank Baum

Produced and Directed by Tony Jones

Performed by the Neighborhood Players, Plymouth, MN

<u>The Cast</u>

Dorothy. . . . . Nancy Thompson

Toto, the dog. . . . . Matt Jones

Scarecrow, Uncle Henry, Munchkin. . . . . Tony Jones

Tin Woodman. . . . . Billy Jones

Cowardly Lion, Munchkin. . . . . Derek Roth

Auntie Em, Wicked Witch of the West, Wizard of Oz. . . . . Faye Levine

The Scarecrow shows Dorothy the Yellow Brick Road.

I produced my own neighborhood plays when I was five years old. I got my friends together and we toured the neighborhood, going from door to door performing short skits and songs.

This year we did a backyard production of *The Wizard of Oz*. Some friends had costumes of their own, but I designed and made most of the costumes, and Nancy and I painted most of the scenery onto old bedsheets that we hung from the swing set.

Dorothy in Munchkin Country

We gathered chairs around the stage and invited
everyone in the neighborhood to be in our audience.
The opening was on a Saturday in August, and it
was the hottest day of the year.

"We're off to see the Wizard"

The Tin Woodman rescues Dorothy.

The Wicked Witch wants both of Dorothy's slippers.

The end of the Wicked Witch of the West

FINALE: "Somewhere over the rainbow"

It seems like everyone goes on summer vacation at
the same time. Anyway, we couldn't find anyone to
play the Wicked Witch of the West until the day
before the opening performance. Then I had to teach
Faye all of her lines in one day. That was about
the hardest thing we had to do for the whole play.
All the rest of it was fun!

61

I'll start dancing again at MDT in September. This fall I'll have five classes a week, and I'll audition to play the lead marionette in *The Nutcracker*. Now that summer's over, I'm getting excited to be studying again. People are always telling me that dancing sounds like a lot of hard work, but the harder I work at it, the more fun I have. I guess I just love to dance.

Here's my whole family in one spot. My dad is Bill
Jones. Billy is my older brother. Matt is my younger
brother. And you met my mom already.